BRIGHT FEAR

T0333455

by the same author
FLÈCHE

MARY JEAN CHAN

Bright Fear

faber

First published in 2023
by Faber & Faber Ltd
The Bindery, 51 Hatton Garden
London EC1N 8HN

Typeset by Hamish Ironside
Printed in the UK by TJ Books Ltd, Padstow, Cornwall

A CIP record for this book is available from the British Library

ISBN 978-0-571-37890-6

Printed and bound in the UK on FSC paper in line with our continuing
commitment to ethical business practices, sustainability and the environment.
For further information see faber.co.uk/environmental-policy

2 4 6 8 10 9 7 5 3

Contents

Who can invent a new fear?

ANNE CARSON

La terre nous aimait un peu je me souviens.

RENÉ CHAR

preface

this spring is colder than winter
loss a resplendent fact those ties
we hold so dear to the living and

the dead I write about this failing
earth since there is softness amid
each grief our bodies repositories

of muscle and memory do not be
afraid let us speak ourselves into
splendour that is the joy I'm after

I. *Grief Lessons*

Bright Fear (I)

During these lengthening days of sunlight
and bright fear, there is too much language,
too little time. I am afraid. I search for desire

indoors, my hands steeped always too long
in soap, then the wetness and the drying,
to allow once more for soiling. Another

faint gesture at the world. I used to dream
about whole days of quiet. Now I seek solace
in sound, replaying Cantopop from the 90s.

On public transport, I keep my staff badge
around my neck, hoping it might ward off
a fist. A young man from Singapore was

beaten for wearing a mask: I can't help
but remember his expression on the six
o'clock news. I enter a classroom feeling

what has come before, its inward twist.
All fear is grief: how my mother wants
me home, how tears come on like poems.

London, 2020

During the early days of the pandemic, they wondered if language meant anything, when it was so clearly the body that faced an existential threat. Keep going, they told their body. One day, they began losing blood. Their period lasted for thirty days. It was the month lockdown ended in the UK, when people flew off on European holidays. Stress, their father once told them, can make you ill. It can make your hair turn white. They looked in the mirror that evening and saw many silvery strands sprouting, like dandelions. The worst thing about this, they confessed to their partner as they lay in bed, is that other people – no matter how much I love them – are all potential hosts. Each night, they would dream about being in a room full of friends, then realise that everyone was unmasked. In the dream, bodies became repugnant. It was in 2003 when they learnt that unseen droplets, breathed gently into air, could kill. People called it SARS. As a teenager, they learnt this English term alongside other words, like sacrifice, sacred, scared.

Hong Kong, 2003

At thirteen, school meant mandatory
medical kits: two face masks, a small

bottle of hand sanitiser. We sang
hymns praising the Lord through

our masks, standing far apart
from one another, empty seats

filling the hall. My father left
in an N95, came home late

with its firm outline on his pale
cheeks. All evening I waited for

him to return, so I could feel
his forehead, listen for a cough.

imperfection's school

the day is	truncated
my	mother
thinks	I am her
angel	my lover
is kind	reminds me
she is	dyslexic
a linguistic	charm
those nights	we read
to each other	the book
travelling	back-
and-	forth
between	us
there was no	word
for this	in HK
only *slow*	or *lazy*
for a class	of thirty-
six	the former
means	you're a lost
cause	the latter
try harder	depression
does not	exist
in families	like ours
trust	the doctor
if he is	your father

tutor-kings   milked
our cash   the contract
was never   equal
we were   desperate
for love   children
of the   1990s
born   in Asia's
World City   you are
nothing   without
a cerebral   cortex
the   coloniser's
gaze   is your own

In the Beginning Was the Word

For twelve years, I was told that English was the lingua franca. Imagine being taught to revere a language from the age of six, when children are most willing to please. Prior to 1997, French was an elective of equal standing to Cantonese. A rumour went around that prefects used to patrol the grounds, fining students if they ever spoke to one another in their mother tongue. English at all times, the teachers trilled. Later, I fell in love with English of my own accord. Or did I? Love, when socially accepted, becomes habit. I took home the English Literature prize, would let no one else come close. It became a badge of honour, a symbol of my uniqueness, though I was lonelier than I had ever been. At times, English feels like the best kind of evening light. On other days, English becomes something harder, like a white shield.

Fully Human

Between Zoom calls – I ponder the meaning of silence
Being silenced – is shocking for some – but not for us

Ask the queer child! Ask what she knows about quiet
or the intimate knowledge of a fire alarm – going off

that only she can hear – that no one will believe existed
She leaves for another country – at nineteen – forsaking

the familiar – the family – the sea surrounding the fragrant
city – departure was once urgent – necessary – and fraught

Try living in the romanticised elsewhere – the sensation
of being watched – is daily and casual – try feeling unsafe

on public transport – try being seated at the same table as
the esteemed scholar – who insists on sharing his expertise

How the British brought so much – to a city he will never
visit – culture, language, the law – my clipped diction fills

the one lull as he refills his glass – to be a diverse thing –
are you listening – some days – all I want – is to go back

Bright Fear (II)

The birds had their tongues tied to silver strings as they hung
mid-air in silence. I was kneeling on the wet earth, crying out.
A disembodied voice informed me that nectar was being slowly
harvested from their throats. The heat from their flailing bodies
pressed my eyes into my skull. I tried to hold myself together in
the dream but could not. Once I was awake, I didn't feel tender.
The brutality of all architecture stunned me wherever I looked.
What were we, as a species, doing? I finally summoned the will
to write *Life* on my to-do list but kept postponing the task. I had
been dreaming of the dying because I could not ignore the news
from home. This viral uncertainty keeping me afraid of intimacy.
Even the bright air felt menacing. A persistent cough developed,
as if to taunt me. My father emails to reassure that all is well at
the clinic, reminds me he went through the SARS epidemic and
never took a day off work. I've inherited a cruel Calvinist ethic.
Today I return to where breath feels possible. My therapist asks,
what is your fantasy? I think to myself: mother's gaze / straight
gaze / male gaze / white gaze . . . I am mortified to admit a dream
about being reborn as the brother, the beloved son, the patriarch.
I want to see this torso in a different light (to beam on it a kinder
gaze) as I wait for something to give. There is fire on the streets
of a city I love and flames in the Arctic, but we must go on living.
Had I imagined this intimate scene: a mother lying at the feet of
her child, begging for a miracle, or was it the other way around?

Love for the Living

What does it mean to want to live? Only this:
to refuse to see the mouth's anguish as a sign

to step out of an open window. To refuse to be
thirty and afraid of leaving one city for another.

To refuse to be a bomb shelter for your mother's
fears. What is it like to believe the years are not

a life sentence for bodies like yours? Like this:
a spiral of rainbow bunting sprung like relief

across a lit sky. The ache when your father
mentions your partner's name. How you'd

notice, incredulous, the way no one cares as
you stand in the open, holding her, kissing.

Answer

At the Poetry Café, some-
    one sipping tea once stared
        at me from across the room

and asked, are you a man or
    a woman? I want to know.
        I got up, moved my laptop,

book and coffee. I eventually
    replied, I would prefer not
        to answer that. Excuse me.

In deep autumn, on a busy
    London street, I want to
        summon myself to be free.

EDI for Migrants (I)

in a pixelated sea of faces   mine remains conspicuous   the mere sight of me
is sufficient to warrant commentary   the moderator says my name   asks if
I am the Chinese partner   joining the call from China   there is a momentary
pause   I tell her I am a senior lecturer   who teaches poetry   at this university
she laughs   says it's good to check one's assumptions!   our training begins
no one else   is invited   to introduce themselves on-screen   the following
minutes are a blur   my mouth a familiar closet   I have locked myself into
my sudden shame   a subcutaneous blush   truthfully speaking   I am tired
of speaking into an expectant silence   weary of having to wield   this tongue
forcefully to ensure my words land   softly and politely to let her off the hook

Sestina

It happened again – the way life happens – my Chinese
face struck like the glow of a torch on a white question:
why is your English so good, the compliment uncertain
of itself. The speaker expects a reply, but I do not know
if his attention will hold for a six-minute history lesson
so I say you're so kind and keep the conversation going.

All this occurs in a safe, queer space. We're about to go
out for pizza, want to join us? I stood next to a Chinese
student who looked at me as if I were a mirror. Lesson
#1: don't mingle only with other Asians. Her questions
were half-hearted, there were white folk to get to know
and I didn't wish to stop her, our camaraderie uncertain

in the fading light as I saw what she saw. The uncertainty
of existing in a historically white space was always going
to haunt me in this gleaming city, where I begin to know
myself. What do you see? Why does it matter? A Chinese
word I learnt as a child, 忍, means to endure, his question
like a blade hovering over a heart. Years go by. The lesson

rises like bread, how I stopped eating rice, a common lesson
imbibed by an expatriate wanting to belong on no uncertain
terms. I longed to please and impress, to cease the questions
concerning my impeccable English, how my accent is going
to ripen over time. I drank your language like tea: Chinese
is no longer a texture I dream in. I left my home knowing

little about the countries we were told to revere, but know
that I have now seen too much for my soul to bear, lessons
that go beyond racial capitalism or an aversion to a Chinese
presence in a room where I am asked to prove my uncertain
right to speak your tongue, to eat a lychee without us going
into too much detail about exotic fruit. Why is the question

never about history, how yours became mine? The questions
we don't dare to touch in daylight or in our sleep . . . we know
like the bitter dregs of coffee. Dear friend, are we ever going
to say what we mean? I fell in love with poetry, those lessons
I sucked like foreign sweets, savouring the sharp uncertainty
of syntax, sound and sense. Multilingual mouths are Chinese.

In love with both English and Chinese, I dreamed of going
abroad to study the answers to Life's question: hard lessons
of the heart. I value frank uncertainty over firm knowledge.

EDI for Migrants (II)

At a Chinese New Year cultural awareness event, I was simultaneously relieved and disappointed that the audience was predominately East Asian. Afterwards, I spoke to a nice, white woman who told me she never knew ESEA people faced racism in this country. How I had proven otherwise, and she was appreciative. In that moment, I thought to myself: I'd rather be doing something else. Something that made me joyful, like watching my partner paint, admiring a tabby cat dozing under a silver birch, or calling my mother, who might ask me how the reading went, if I spoke clearly, whether anyone clapped, and for how long?

resolve

come home to
this body, this
unhomeliness

masquerading
under a pile of
laundry (where

your birthmark
lingers) dearest
one day you will

feel free to cut
your hair lush
like knotweed

a head crowned
in the lightness
of summer light

EDI for Migrants (III)

post-colony is a state of mind
it is reaching deep into the past
as you sit on a BA flight travelling

across a genteel English landscape
and history not reaching back
neo-colony is a state of being

it is the illusion of freedom
until it is withdrawn ever so
softly like a hospital curtain

the more you successfully
assimilate the more you see
the terms and conditions feel

the texture of abstract nouns
Equality Diversity Inclusion

Last Summer

You on the balcony of a condo in Queenstown to escape
the aircon's onslaught, me sullen from the blistering heat,

wishing you would come inside. Earlier, we avoided
holding hands on the MRT. In the afternoon light,

a straight couple kissed and we noticed. You swim
laps as the poem you recited on our first date pools

like torrential rain in my mind. The palm trees
remain their centred selves, the roads dark from

weather. At Changi airport, we fight and reconcile.
I get you a new charger, you show me the rooftop

cactus garden. In the gallery of memory, we are
happy. It is closing time. You have already left.

Circles

I am not familiar with rivers,
          but during those months of bubbles
when I did not hold anyone close,

I took to wandering along
          a stretch of the River Lea which
several species of bird inhabited.

I watched and watched until even
          the water seemed to recognise me,
the same coots, those shimmering

shapes their slender and agile torsos
          made: the same form I had glimpsed
one spring morning on a friend's

wall after lockdown had lifted:
          Wassily Kandinsky's *Several Circles*,
a form he saw as the synthesis

of the greatest oppositions.
          When I couldn't sleep or wake,
I was saved by geometry:

a commotion of coots convincing
          me to withstand the quotidian tug-
of-war between terror and love.

II. *Ars Poetica*

I

The poet opened a clean Word document, titled it *POETRY*, then saved it in a folder titled *NONFICTION*, then saved it in a folder titled *FICTION*.

II

When I was young, I realised my body
was something to be held back or kept
in its place, so I have mastered the art
of observation, how to watch faces for
a frown or grimace: signs of weather.

Once, a teacher came up to me in the
school playground and asked me if I
had any feelings. Your expression is
blank, she added. What could I say?
I knew how to dim any spark within.

Years later, I left home for the poem:
inscrutable house, constructed space,
blue room, how the poets have named
a heaven in which lonely meanings sit
companionably beside lonely children.

III

The novel feels like a springer spaniel running off-
leash the poem a warm basket it returns to always

As a teenager I learnt to minimise myself whenever
my father's face transformed into a furious sunset

What does it feel like to not have to hide things like
a small splinter of sadness or an even smaller need?

I work too well with constraints so I cannot enjoy
the sheer amount of space a prose writer deserves

My therapist says it has to do with my relationship
to freedom something I find just as trying as prose

I want my reader to understand my protagonist and
their feelings without my having to describe them in

detail the way a poet I adore once wrote about her
brother a gate and a cheese and mustard sandwich

IV

at eighteen, you were as far   away from poetry
as you now are   from the sea
a man once   asked you where
you found grace   you told him in a poem

for years you thought   touch was the tap
running   your fingers braiding
the soft water   or the shower spilling
incandescently   over a shamed torso

at an airport in Texas   a barista playfully asked
if you were a professional   tennis player
praising your shoulders   you were
in transit to attend   a slam poetry contest

yet you felt seen somehow   so you cleaved to that
small identity   all afternoon
comforted you had a place   in that brutal country
later that summer   you returned home

as yourself   so much lighter now
then left once more   clutching a slim book close
on the long flight   to London
each word a warm   hand to keep you

from the edge of things   each line a hum
to bring back   the hallelujah

V

On my weekly commute to Oxford, whiteness greets me
as a kind of stopping device. I cease to drink from my
orange juice as two white men sit opposite me. I try not
to assume anything, to continue to inhabit a space of
equals. Those Chinese tourists . . . you can go into a lift
in Bicester Village and hear more than three languages
these days, makes you wonder whether you are in
England at all. His companion laughs and nods. I stare
at my iPhone, sip my juice. Perhaps my face is a sign
they cannot – have chosen not to – decipher. There is a
poem I wish I could have written, in which a powerful
conversation ensues between us, where the speaker of
the poem speaks up. Instead, I reach for the only book
I have with me that day, the title of which I cannot
remember. You should know it was a novel written in
English. There is a flicker in his eyes I cannot help but
recognise. He pauses, turns the conversation elsewhere.

VI

I am a poet, I said to my inner child, their perennial flowering
of queerphobic introjections.

I am a poet, I said to my hometown, whose love I once had
sufficient reason to doubt.

I am a poet, I said to the many wild mouths from which micro-
aggressions and harms flow.

I am a poet, I said to the world's rage, its grief. Now I offer this
in return, the way trees do.

VII

I have been trained to plunder my own
thoughts, exploit my deepest resources,
but I am told that a poem is a wandering

little drift of unidentified sound, which led
me back to the most important thing I had
learnt recently: what my partner said to me

about the red-hot poker, how I might pay
attention to the vivid logic of its colours,
as we paused to look, and I tried to listen.

VIII

Perhaps poetry is nothing
but a struggle to translate
the weight of flesh against
bone into syllables that
sound the shape
of things:
leaf
light
tree
sky
the fact
of your face,
beautiful like breath.

IX

It is 4.30 p.m. and pitch-black but we love each other.
This is enough to keep me inside the poem, during
days of lost epiphanies and great pain. Scarry notes
that pain isn't 'of' or 'for' anything, it is itself alone.
There is no language for it, so the birds of metaphor
won't rest here, won't give me a swan or a sign that
things will be better. It is dark outside. We remain.

X

I am constantly chastising myself for leaning too hard
on someone else, particularly since I am used to being

a brick wall for others, one that never yields no matter
the pressure being exerted. Then I came across a poem,

'Edward Hopper's *Office at Night*', where the poet writes:
I cannot take care of everyone on some nights I wake in

a panic . . . soon I vowed in dreams to cease absorbing my
partner's feelings like chlorophyll does sunlight, even as

my father asks me over email why I've stopped practising
Chinese calligraphy: the only thing he has ever explicitly

asked of me. I am reminded of another poet's experience
of love, with its austere and lonely offices, and a solemn

father who seldom speaks. I am reading another's words
to ask what I cannot ask: have I been there for my father?

XI

This is the myth of love's tenderness:
that it only heals and cannot wound.
After thirty years of spinning around
in space, you hear echoes, wilderness
among stars devoid of human tempers.
Linger there – it is quiet – your breath
audible as the staccato burn on a hearth.
Dear reader, how often are you tempted
to infidelity with words: those curious
shapes that simply demand you listen?
Offer a translation your life can bear.
Revisit poems that spark mysterious
doorways in the mind and glistening
eyes. Let ink seep into what you hear.

XII

my poetry students don't know
they've saved me, the lecturer
who is supposed to talk about

grief and mothers and queer
joy or shame with a sense of
critical distance, except I am

nearly moved to display deep
emotion when they read their
poems aloud, as I realise why

I value being in a small room
housed in the business school
each Thursday doing the hard

work of mending or mourning
what remains dear to each of us

XIII

As a child, I often considered the impact that falling
in love with English had on my mother's happiness.
She once said, don't think you can talk back to me in
a colonial language, it isn't superior! I can't describe

her voice – when she speaks in Shanghainese – it is
sweet like water. Her language came to me as in a
familiar dream, a lotus flower sinking into my self
and blooming. During my first month in England,

I learnt the art and science of speaking to reassure.
How else can I survive? It's so easy to be ashamed.
I am asked why my poems are so clear. I'll confess:
it's what happens when you want to be understood.

Ten years ago, I found myself in Nice and learnt to
dream in French, my mother's first foreign tongue.
That summer, the sea was also my mother, the Bay
of Angels held me in its polyphony, and I chose all

my loves – Cantonese, English, Mandarin, French –
spoke with a satisfaction I had not felt in years, saw
my relationship to the world through sounds again,
till I was reconciled, the way rainbows exist in rain.

XIV

According to Sara Ahmed, race is a rather queer matter when one considers how whiteness is invisible and unmarked as the absent centre against which others appear only as lines of deviation. I am reminded of Ahmed's words during a poetry reading, when an audience member asks me to perform a poem in Chinese. In that moment, my race becomes a queer matter. In a poem about postcolonial grief, the speaker remains queer. Billy-Ray Belcourt: poetry is creaturely. It resists categorical capture. It is a shape-shifting, defiant force in the world. The queer poem is also future-oriented. José Esteban Muñoz: we have never been queer, yet queerness exists for us as an ideality that can be distilled from the past and used to imagine a future. The queer poem, then, is hopeful. As I write, the queer poem is a wish which stems from a desire.

XV

I cherish books because my mother first
loved them. My grandfather found her
a Chinese translation of Percy Bysshe
Shelley's poems and Charles Dickens'
Great Expectations in a time of famine.
What my mother taught me was how
to revere the light language emitted.
My mother perceived that Literature
was precious harvest from wild fields
of sorrow: a stanza I'd someday read
like those water reeds glinting under
the Canterbury sun that summer we
visited, each line clear as a reflection,
each syllable robust enough for a life.

XVI

Home, my therapist suggests, is where
you don't have to explain yourself.
Where is that place? Perhaps
here is home, in the long poem
of our lives. Where she offers me
a cup of freshly brewed
oolong tea, and I am moved
by the scent of something
bittersweet. Where our thoughts
spill over as I adore the warmth
in your voice. Where the afternoon
light is so kind, and the corgi lies
fast asleep at our feet. Where I begin
to speak, and you hear me, unequivocally.

III.   *Field Notes on a Family*

Hindsight

All the ingredients necessary for happiness:
I grew up well-fed, years away from
conflict and its aftermath.
When someone in the family knows
sacrifice as the only currency,
such knowledge seeps.
History must suffice.
My mother knew hunger. Bread, in the absence of
a miracle, cannot yield more loaves.
I will give myself the mango's stone,
save the sweet flesh for someone else.

Save the sweet flesh for someone else:
I will give myself the mango's stone.
A miracle cannot yield more loaves.
My mother knew hunger. Bread, in the absence of
history, must suffice.
Such knowledge seeps:
sacrifice as the only currency
when someone in the family knows
conflict and its aftermath.
I grew up well-fed, years away from
all the ingredients necessary for happiness.

fireworks on the tongue

and yes I bit into the turbot sautéed in herb oil and yes I made
the conscious choice to be pescatarian in spite of those tragic
documentaries about farmed salmon and yes I craved the
smell of burnt meat and yes I could not miss the homeless
man sitting outside La Petite Maison and yes I called an Uber
for us to return home and yes home is a nice apartment in East
London and yes I read an article on Korean dystopian fiction
in translation and felt better for it and yes I slept that night in
a bed with only me in it and yes my partner had stayed that
week in an Airbnb in order that my parents might visit me in
peace and yes I am still trying to achieve my way into love and
yes I cried when my mother told me to take care of her since
it has been so long and yes the turbot it was so moist it was so
soft and yes fine dining has forever been a social lubricant in
my family and yes without fireworks on the tongue to distract
us into harmony there would have been all the love we could
muster or a desolation none of us could have withstood

Glance

You are four, five, six,
seven, eight, nine, ten
and refusing to wear
a dress again. How
a body endures
the toll of
another's
glance.

In the flat, speech
unravels like smoke.
Outside, the moon
is losing its mind.

Her mouth was a gate
you unbolted. You run
onto the street. The lights
are sweet, honeycombed.

She promised
that a mother's
love was the one
unsinkable ship.
You remember this
as you wander into
the blue hours between
reckoning and breakfast.

brother (I)

brother, brother, where have you been
(I lost two of you, one after another)
when I was twelve, my mum told me
she was about to adopt another, she
broke the news casually after I had
come home from school, she offered
me a biscuit, I took a moment, then
replied in my most grown-up voice:
when will I meet him (I thought to
myself, I am not a boy) but the next
week she had changed her mind: you
receded from my life like hard weather

beauty

even in our fiercest rage
my mother and I were
devoted we stayed and
fought since we could
not be disloyal always
the same cause a dress
a pair of heels my hair

when father came home
he would find us meek
subdued pretending no
calamity had ever struck
at night I would envision
something strange once
my dream involved a boy

standing at some sea's edge
waiting for a miracle in the
shape of a lone blue whale
all I remember of the rest
is that we were saved and
I awoke feeling as if I could
continue living in this body

Calling Home

Her voice flows through your soul like air. You steady your voice, but she knows to ask about the tightness in your throat. After all that has happened, have you finally forgiven each other? The child asks: how long will it feel like burning. Your mother wants to know what you had for lunch, tells you what she ate for dinner. This mutual exchange of images. You ask her to turn on her camera so you can see her, knowing she will refuse. Another day, she says. How to tell her that after decades on earth, you should be able to know each other. That what children want is for their parents to see them, as they already are. Instead, you are sent photos of yourself: an eight-year-old in a beige dress at a wedding, an awkward teenager dressed for the opera in Milan on your first trip to Europe. How to tell her: none of those versions fit anymore. Your partner walks into the room. You are reminded that you cannot change those you love most, your voice blue in the violet hour.

brother (II)

brother, brother, neither of you came
after I'd arrived my mother could not

bear those long days when I behaved
too much like a boy the plastic sword

I brandished after school the irrefutable
proof one day she asked if I had wanted

to be her only child I wanted you to live
would have borrowed your shirts if you

had let me opened fire in video games
even though I cannot stand any form

of violence what happens to the mother
who could not mourn her miscarriages

what happens to the child who escaped
unscathed and is now burdened to live

bout

at fencing camp in Guangzhou   sleeping with our heads   facing each other
on top bunks   at the local university dormitory   I feel you shift   imagine

our fingertips touching   think to myself   that this is the closest I will get
to love   something so alive and present   yet irrevocably distant in the dark

the next day we fly   to Shanghai   for the Nationals   I lose my first bout
only to find you alone   in the stands   distraught   at having been beaten

my body moves   till your head   rests like a robin on my shoulder   we sit
in silence for a while   then a sudden sharp pain   on my neck   I turn to see

my mother   who has flown here   to watch me   the robin on my shoulder
is gone   *Let me*   my mother eventually says   filling the space between us

Quiet

Wonder what songs are left
after the mothers have gone
to bed and the whole world
is lighter without their grief.

Reunion

One night, I dream of a hotel in Bloomsbury where my mother hands me a USB flash drive, asks me to fill it with images of myself. She says, I want to devour you. You were so tiny once; I could fit your foot into my mouth. My father is busy unpacking, so I make small talk as my mother stares at me, the way she stares whenever she hasn't seen my face for a long time. Your hair is too short. In the cab, she continues to look me over from head to toe. I am wearing the watch she gave me for my thirtieth birthday, one I do not usually wear. We dine at a Hunan restaurant on Gerrard Street. I make sure my mother has a hard seat, so her back pain does not flare up. The waiter scribbles furiously on his flimsy wad of paper. The wood ear mushroom salad, salt and pepper prawns and Lanzhou stretched noodles arrive, along with a pot of Iron Buddha tea. My mother loves the handmade noodles, enjoys the cacophony of families. I ask about them. They ask about me. We pretend that I live in London alone.

After Twenty-One Days in Hotel Quarantine

I feel engulfed by the surrounding
sea, by which I mean, my own life.

        Both blue and unfathomable. During
        that first night back in my childhood

bed, a sinking feeling visits
and glows softly like pith in

        the stomach's pit. My mother finds me
        weary in the morning, brimming with

contradictions. I am elated to be free,
yet I alert her to a mysterious pain

        in my abdomen. My father declares
        I'm healthy. Anxiety needs another

name, its diamond-like facets glittering
like far-off explosions on our perilous

        earth. In this city I am ahead of time,
        strung out between two realities like

dreams of rescuing a beloved friend or
being lifted entirely out of depression.

        It is not simple to miss another voice.

A Denim Shirt

Write something cheerful, you and Dad urged, as if
poetry were comedy. What about tragedy, I wanted
to ask, but didn't, because it was hot, and I had not
seen you both for eighteen months. For all of 2020,
I raged inwardly at the measures which kept HK's
borders closed. Flights were forbidden. I wondered
what I was doing here, living in a country that was
home, and yet not quite home. After the travel ban
lifted and twenty-one days passed, I saw your faces
at 1 a.m., your arms waving behind a metal barrier.
In hindsight, I should have been kinder. I said what
I felt I needed to express. Too much honesty can be
a fault, I remind my impatient heart. How to join up
the dots when the pattern was hardly evident. I was
but a child, then. How was I to know that I'd given
birth to a daughter who didn't like wearing dresses,
you wanted to know. I cried, I explain in a soothing,
quiet voice that only adults are capable of. My tears.
That should have been enough. Then I tell you that
I am busy: work as my shield and song. For an hour,
I just looked at the wild, fluorescent sky. Eventually
you called, and said it was time for dinner. And so it
went until it was time for me to leave. Back home in
London, I find a denim shirt tucked around a box of
Godiva chocolates. For you and J, you said. You did
not mention the shirt, the kind you had always told
me never to wear. I thanked you, for the chocolates.

How It Must Be Said

In the 1980s, a manicurist asked my mother where she was originally from. She replied, Shanghai. The woman said, so now you Mainlanders have rice to eat! No more congee I suppose, you are rich enough to afford a manicure. As a television script-writer in HK, my mother wrote in Standard Chinese, but the editor ordered her to acquire Cantonese.

*

After a fight, I sat crying in my room. I had said some things to my mother that hurt her deeply. I was incapable of such fury in English. My father came in to talk to me. He said, you know that Cantonese isn't your mother's native language. I looked at him. What did language have to do with pain? He said, try speaking to her in Shanghainese.

*

Do you want to be liked or seen? My therapist asks. Each year, I migrate between cities and selves. How a familiar voice can make one weep. For my thirty-first, a close friend translates a poem of mine into French, her mother tongue. I am a stubborn beginner in her language, so I surrender to the sensation of being translated, and therefore seen.

*

Plants without roots wither in rain, my mother tells me in a text message. This is a translation, the way I understand my mother in three languages. For over a decade, I have taken what I could bear from the source text and discarded the rest. What do you miss most about HK? A childhood friend asks. Cantonese, I say. How it sounds like summer rain.

The Painter

Last spring, I thought of nothing but the sullen cities, their silence, but overnight you began painting, took colours I had not heard of and made our four walls very much alive. It was so thrilling to learn you all over again: the wash glowing whitely on canvas, the calm movement of your hand. I never knew you'd drawn discreetly as a child. I think my enthusiasm took you by surprise, but I couldn't help it! Very soon the autumn leaves you love will be turning the colour of rust so we'll quietly make our way through an anguished or peaceful hour, holding the year inside our scene, imagined and factual like hope, comforting as fresh grass beneath our toes.

The Translator

Your face looks like the full moon!
my mother observes. We sit down
to eat. Now and again, I translate

her questions for my partner whose
Chinese is a riddle well told. Later,
I bless my feet with aniseed, ginger

and water to ring in the first year
of language no longer meaning
rift or sorrow, but its opposite.

I am a translator: one who is
multilingual, refusing soil
and other forms of burial.

Out

Can I be myself now? I ask
my parents in a dream.
There is a long silence that lasts
for years, punctuated by half-
finished sentences. This is how it is
with family. One day, my mother
said to me on the phone: We are one
body, you know that, right?
She meant me, my father and her.
To disagree was to admit to my desire
for cruelty, this severance
that has allowed me to chisel
a way out. Yesterday,
as we spoke, my parents
looked at me and simply said, yes.
Yes? I asked. Yes, they replied.
We love you. The sentence
was complete, no longer
half-finished. The months
ahead of me are wide open.

postscript

in the penultimate scene where mother
and child are listening to one another

speak in spite of everything the way
an orchestra might play on bravely

even when the audience claps before
it's time you will want to stay awhile

in subtropical winter heat as sunlight
blazes through the fog of memory you

begin to wonder if the origin story can
at last be transfigured into the version

redacted through the centuries (the one
in which the garden comes alive) a queer

child's vision of paradise where the trees
are free to bear their multitudinous light

Notes

The epigraphs are taken respectively from Anne Carson's *Glass, Irony and God*, and from *Selected Poems of René Char*, edited by Mary Ann Caws and Tina Jolas.

'Preface' draws from C. D. Wright's 'Key Episodes from an Earthly Life'.

'Bright Fear (I)' began as part of an invited submission for Manchester Metropolitan University's 'Write Where We Are Now' project.

'Fully Human' is partly inspired by Cathy Park Hong's *Minor Feelings*.

'Bright Fear (II)' was commissioned for Poets & Players in Manchester on the theme of 'Altered Nature'.

'Ars Poetica (II)' contains phrases from Elizabeth Bishop, W. S. Graham and Anne Carson.

'Ars Poetica (III)' refers to 'The Gate' by Marie Howe.

'Ars Poetica (V)' draws upon Sara Ahmed's formulation of whiteness from *Queer Phenomenology: Orientations, Objects, Others*.

'Ars Poetica (VII)' includes a description of poetry taken from Mary Ruefle's *Madness, Rack, and Honey: Collected Lectures*.

'Ars Poetica (IX)' includes a line from Elaine Scarry's *The Body in Pain: The Making and Unmaking of the World*.

'Ars Poetica (X)' includes lines from 'Edward Hopper's *Office at Night*' by Victoria Chang and 'Those Winter Sundays' by Robert Hayden.

'Ars Poetica (XIV)' is a collage poem interspersed with my own words, containing quotations from Ahmed's *Queer Phenomenology*, Billy-Ray Belcourt's *This Wound Is a World* and José Esteban Muñoz's *Cruising Utopia: The Then and There of Queer Futurity*.

'Ars Poetica (XVI)' was partly inspired by Emily Berry's meditation on light in *Unexhausted Time*.

'Hindsight' uses the specular form, invented by Julia Copus.

'Calling Home' quotes from Anne Carson's 'Lines' and T. S. Eliot's 'The Waste Land'.

'The Painter' uses the end words of the opening lines in Sylvia Plath's 'Mushrooms'. It is written in the form of a golden shovel, invented by Terrance Hayes in homage to Gwendolyn Brooks. This poem is dedicated to Jo.

'Out' repeats the phrase 'half-finished sentence(s)', taken from Carson's 'The Glass Essay'.

'postscript' is inspired in part by Seamus Heaney's 'Postscript'. This poem is dedicated to my mother.

Acknowledgements

Previous versions of some of these poems have appeared in the following publications: *London Review of Books, Granta, New Republic, HEAT* (Giramondo Publishing), *East Side Voices* (Sceptre, 2022), *New Statesman, Five Dials, Poetry Review, bath magg, Visual Verse, INQUE, Poetry Birmingham Literary Journal, Oxford Review of Books, A Hurry of English* (ignitionpress, 2018) and the Academy of American Poets 'Poem-a-Day' series.

I wish to thank Oxford Brookes for a 2021/22 Research Excellence Award, which gave me time to reflect and write. Heartfelt thanks to Emma Paterson for believing in me. Thank you to Matthew Hollis, Lavinia Singer and Robert Hampson for their editorial feedback and encouragement. I am grateful to Enora Lessinger, Niall Munro, Will Harris, Anthony (Vahni) Capildeo, Andrew McMillan, Kaitlin Chan, Tiff Mak, Johanna de Vos and Min Sern Teh for their inspiration and friendship. As ever, this book is dedicated to my parents for their love and support.